CENZONTLE

WINNER, 2017 A. POULIN, JR. POETRY PRIZE
SELECTED BY BRENDA SHAUGHNESSY

WINNER OF THE A. POULIN, JR. POETRY PRIZE

CENZONTLE

POEMS

Marcelo Hernandez Castillo

FOREWORD BY BRENDA SHAUGHNESSY

A. POULIN, JR. NEW POETS OF AMERICA SERIES, NO. 40

BOA EDITIONS, LTD. ☙ ROCHESTER, NY ☙ 2018

First Edition
20 21   7 6 5 4 3

For information about permission to reuse any material from this book, please contact The
Permissions Company at www.permissionscompany.com or e-mail permdude@gmail.com.

Publications by BOA Editions, Ltd.—a not-for-profit corporation under section
501 (c) (3) of the United States Internal Revenue Code—are made possible with
funds from a variety of sources, including public funds from the Literature
Program of the National Endowment for the Arts; the New York State Council **ART WORKS.**
on the Arts, a state agency; and the County of Monroe, NY. Private funding   arts.gov
sources include the Lannan Foundation for support of the Lannan Translations
Selection Series; the Max and Marian Farash Charitable Foundation; the Mary   State of the Arts
S. Mulligan Charitable Trust; the Rochester Area Community Foundation; the
Steeple-Jack Fund; the Ames-Amzalak Memorial Trust in memory of Henry Ames,   **NYSCA**
Semon Amzalak, and Dan Amzalak; and contributions from many individuals nationwide. See Colo-
phon on page 108 for special individual acknowledgments.

Cover Design: Sandy Knight
Cover Art: "Empty Nest" by Lisette Chavez
Interior Design and Composition: Richard Foerster
Manufacturing: McNaughton & Gunn
BOA Logo: Mirko

Library of Congress Cataloging-in-Publication Data

Names: Hernandez Castillo, Marcelo, 1988– author
Title: Cenzontle : poems / by Marcello Hernandez Castillo.
Description: First edition. | Rochester, NY : BOA Editions, Ltd., 2018. |
  Series: New poets of America series ; No. 40
Identifiers: LCCN 2017044816 | ISBN 9781942683537 (pbk. : alk. paper)
Classification: LCC PS3608.E76845 A6 2018 | DDC 811/.6—dc23
LC record available at https://lccn.loc.gov/2017044816

BOA Editions, Ltd.
250 North Goodman Street, Suite 306
Rochester, NY 14607
www.boaeditions.org
A. Poulin, Jr., Founder (1938–1996)

For Julián.
For Rubi.

Contents

FOREWORD

I find myself speechless as I endeavor to write an introduction to this book of poems. I don't want to say anything, really. When I first fell into these poems I was unprepared. Nobody told me what to expect or that I wouldn't emerge as I was before. Nobody held my hand. I fell head first into a whole new language, a new music, a new vision of love and loss and dispossession and reclamation. Why would I want to warn anybody of the miraculous? And, further, why on earth would I want to ruin it by talking? I want to listen to these poems echo and sing and let the songs etch me into a new form, a new species of heart-haver. Who talks over beautiful music? Who doesn't yearn to be dissolved, breathless, in the deep, dark waters of true art?

But a reader mustn't give in to this drowning, to this ecstasy. A reader can't merely receive passively, however grateful s/he is. Readers must speak back, find their tongues, when a book sings this powerfully. As a reader, I know this book changed me. The book itself knows change, how to change itself, knows so well how transformation—vast essential change which would seem to oppose a self—brings a person ever closer to their truth. "The song becoming the bird becoming the song" as Marcelo Hernandez Castillo says, binding the question of how we are to how we are continually becoming. It is mesmerizing and miraculous to read a poet who becomes and is and remembers and knows and does not tell but reverberates (in threnody, harmony, syncopation, cacophony) that knowledge and that memory.

Song comes from grief and love that lingers, mutates, is absorbed. Castillo knows that blood (a white belt, a cancer, a lover's, a legacy) is a lyric never to be forgotten: *"It's in your blood, / which means / it's all of you."* And song comes from rage, demanding justice, in which compassion is not meant to forgive but to remember, to inscribe, to know by heart. And in case anyone forgets, the poet seems to say, the cenzontle doesn't. The bird sings what it hears, is a historical record, and becomes its song. It is in the cenzontle, after all, ("Perhaps the butterflies are mute because / no one would believe their terrible stories.") that we hear ourselves. All the selves we can bear to carry inside of us ("We closed our eyes / and looked for each other") or the selves we mirror for each other in desire and love ("I leaned into you / all of you, / as if in chorus.") or the selves we shed or lost or abandoned only to be face to face in some other form ("The bones / unhinged at the same speed / as the branches.")

This is just a description. This is not an introduction. It's impossible to write "an introduction" to this book of poems because it already knows you, reader. Castillo is a poet who can say "I will believe in anything you do not / and bring it to you" and deliver with such grace and power you merge with the page, not passively, not submissively, but in recognition. Recognition—to re-know—is an odd word and one that is not quite right. I don't have the right words here, as I said. What I am writing here is a note to you, reader, as you enter this book. Not warning or spoiler or explanation or voucher, just a loving note. My note merely aims to say that I emerged from this book in silence, in awe, with gratitude, and have yet to give name to its immensity. Reader, should you join me in believing this virtuosic poet and what he has to say, his music which is history and his song which is memory, "years from now / there will be a name/ for what you and I are doing."

—Brenda Shaughnessy

CENZONTLE

"Emptiness is a thing that grows by being moved."
—Jean Toomer

Cenzontle

Because the bird flew before
     there was a word
     for flight

          years from now
          there will be a name
       for what you and I are doing.

     I licked the mango of the sun—

     between its bone and its name
     between its color and its weight

       the night was heavier
       than the light it hushed.

Pockets of unsteady light.

       The bone—
       the seed
    inside the bone—

          the echo
       and its echo
       and its shape.

     Can you wash me without my body
     coming apart in your hands?

Call it *wound*—
call it *beginning*—

The bird's beak twisted
into a small circle of awe.

You called it cutting apart,
I called it song.

I.

ORIGIN OF DROWNING OR CROSSING THE RIO BRAVO

We don't even remember
what we look like anymore.

Down here, everything is wrapped
in cloth and tied with yarn.

     The light
     inching through the swell—

     our backs glossy
     as a tooth dipped in honey.

Sometimes I want to climb down a tree in secret.
I want to stand in front of a crowd
and whisper a speech in secret.

     If they can kiss you,
     they can kill you.

You're a star, honey,
everyone wants your picture.

＊

We've done this before.

We've played every couple in every movie
rubbing makeup on our faces that smears underwater.

      You keep stuffing my plastic face
in your plastic mouth
thinking this will all make it better.

It might.

              What if we rose
          above the water
          where the moon wraps
                its legs around a man
                too old to care?

＊

I'm only saying what you want to hear.
You've heard every variation before.
      Nothing happens twice.

      Nothing
      happens
      twice.

＊

There isn't anything interesting up there.
Only young lovers brimming over
with extinct longing.

Everything has a shadow and a yawn.
        Twiceness is not a thing of this world.

                    ⤳

Be still, our children will come.

        If you happen to come across someone,
        and if they ask, say
        he's just playing dead.

                And then you'll believe it yourself
                and will light a candle for me.

        Nothing will convince you that prayer is a removal of self—
                    a distancing.

        Let's continue this drowning
to remember what we look like.

            Let's keep waking underwater
            until one of us gets it right.

Go ahead, sharpen yourself against these rocks.

        Dress me in all your wet clothes.

Immigration Interview with Don Francisco

In the church was the deepest
well of the city where the priest
was lowered every morning.

[*Please say more*   ]

I've split open the small fish
and counted the candles tucked inside—
all the pink nails tapping the wicks.

[*Please elaborate*   ]

If I had children,
there would be no reason
to empty the bowls
stagnant with rain water—
no reason at all to keep saying
"you are almost."

[*Please say more*   ]

The wasps: their multitude of clapping hands.

[*Please elaborate*   ]

How small the dolls.
How insignificant
the hands that move them.

[*Please say more*   ]

Perhaps the butterflies are mute because
no one would believe their terrible stories.

ESPARTO, CALIFORNIA

Each pepper field is the same.
        In each one I am a failed anthem.

I don't know English
        but there is so little
        that needs translated out here.

For twelve hours I have picked
the same colored pepper.

Still, I don't know what country
does death belong to.

My skin is peeling.

        ¿Cual dios quisiera ser fuente?

If only I could choose what hurt.

An inheritance.

        Those lost mothers bound
        to the future of their blood.

I am walking again through the footage
where the white dress loses its shape.

Even moving my hands to sort
        the peppers is a kind of running.

Hold still.

The child will sing because I was once her flag.

      She will take my picture
            —both groom and bride—
      a country she has never seen.

I will give her the knife
to make her own camera.

The gift of shade and water—
        the likeness of a star to possess.

And I am only half sick
      if being sick
is just a bone waiting to harden.

      I could be a saint
since there exists no pleasure
that wasn't first abandoned to us out of boredom.
We traffic in the leftovers of ecstasy.

How lonely and inventive those angels were.

      If I could speak their language,
I would tell them all my real name

    —Antonia—

And with my curved knife,
I would rid them of all their failures.

El Frutero

Apá likes his fruit sweeter than his women.

I imagine Apá growing a garden
in the next room though I know he is not.

I imagine Apá holding my mother's face beneath him
and slowly parting its earth for a plum orchard.

I open the door.
I know I'm supposed to look
away from his reaping.

My mother's face a blue
only known to exist in seeds.
Her limp body flapping with air.

I am young.
It is early.
She smiles at me and I don't look away—

her eyelids opening long enough
for me to see the ripeness
his hands are capable
of tending.

After he leaves, I gently gather
the plums of her eyes
and tuck them
in my pocket and put her to sleep.

I walk to a field
and bury them somewhere far,
so he will never find them.

When I return, I rub salt all over her body
so not a single blossom will ever grow there again.

[Condition] :

Before the wasp, a hammer. Before the hammer, a knot.

All the violins hushed in their cases.

He is. Then she is. Then he is.

When the knot is untied, he will no longer feel
the shape of the dark with his hands.

The corridor of blood
stuck in its hum—
a lullaby in the policeman's radio.

When it resembles a child, she will see through the child.

She will strap the child to her back
and expand the light around her.

She will dream.

She will swing the hammer at anything that moves.

She says *try it motherfucker.*

Then the cold particular to street lamps,
or the bird given over to shadow,
or just after.

She will laugh and the child will laugh with her.

[Portrait] :

In the field of onions
Amá's eyes have blossomed—
        hanging from the petals,
        and she, so far away,

unable to blink

wondering
where so much color could possibly come from.

[Condition] :

She called the cops.
But it was too late.

If she opened the door?
If she looked through the window?

The TV with its jokes and the baby crying on the floor uncontrollably.

She didn't look, she collected the reward
and bought a gun.

She loaded the gun and fixed the man in the story.

But it wasn't the same,
so she broke her promise again
and returned the gun
but the store wouldn't take it
because they tested it out back and said it was still capable of measure.

She bought another gun
and the clerk smiled
as if she were buying roses,
which she was,
and she said it was *special*, it was *real special*.

She went home
and gave him the roses,
but it wasn't the same.

The clocks stopped working
and the cops returned with their dogs
but they wouldn't believe her.

They said *It'd be a shame you know, a real shame.*
She said *please* but she could no longer point.

[Portrait] : [Deportation]

He's in the show for the woman in the mirror.

Or, she *is* the show
and *he* is the mirror.

Between them a door.
She swore it would open—

the white and the blue and the white again
as if everything's on trial, which it is.

The judge.   The witness.

The lion climbing the window
into the orchard without being seen.

The orchard where they are both lost and found again.

WETBACK

After the first boy called me a wetback,
I opened his mouth and fed him a spoonful of honey.

     I like the way you say "honey," he said.

I made him a necklace out of the bees that have died in my yard.

       How good it must have felt before the small village
       echoed its grief in his throat; before the sirens began ringing.

How fallow their scripture.

Perhaps we were on stage which meant it was a show,
which meant our only definition of a flower was also a flower.

I waved to the crowd
like they taught me,
like a mini-miss something.

      Thank you.
      Thank you.

Yes, I could have ripped open his throat.
I could have blown him a kiss from the curtain.

I wanted to dance by myself in a dark room
filled with the wingless bodies of bees—

to make of this our own Old Testament
with all the same beheaded kings
        pointing at all the same beheaded prophets.

The same Christ running through every door
like a man who forgot his child in the car.

But the lights were too bright.
I couldn't hear him because I wasn't on stage.

        I could have been anyone's
        idea of pity.

How quiet our prophets.
        Let my bare back remind him of every river he's swam in.

Miel and *miel.*

        I pulled the bees off the string
        and cupped them in my palm.

I told him my Spanish name.

There was nothing dry on my body—
The lamps falling over in the dark of me.

Dear Ramón

—Zacatecas, México 1959

It was not your fault the ranch burned.
Did you watch the horses inside?

All the dark stones on their tongues.

The mares with their slow whines
louder than the making of honey up close.

       The next morning,
    after the night wrestled the fire
    into a placid hush,

you walked back
to what was left of the stable.

       You knew
      those bodies
    to be the bodies of horses.

     The glint of a tooth
nestled in ash was the single
brightest thing in that field.

CENTURY OF GOOD METAL WITH THREE PRAYERS

My skin is darker
than the flag burning
in the man's mouth.

> *Soy acampanado,*
> *rezando por las entrañas.*

Everything is larger
than the mothers robbed of grief.
Everything is to the left of them.

> *Padre Santo que estas en el cielo.*

But who am I to the guns
painted for the young?

How large the paper kites
have grown over their faces,
as if the riddle
was meant to be answered.

> *Los pasos de su boca.*
> *Las tijeras de su santo.*

Let this be the last time
a boy like me cuts himself open,

trying to find the swans
flapping their wings inside him.

Let this be the last time they appear,
unfolding their large wings in his chest.

And he will not move,
as if to say *I will not hurt you,*
afraid the smallest breath
will scare them away.

Sugar

My father's hands split peaches in half and fed me.

Mouth / and nail.
Salt and / a little piss.

Always the leather, always / my ass bleeding with welts—
my ass purple with love,

always / the belt he called Daisy.
And I said *hello Daisy*, / and she said *hello*.

And *he*, / bent over the sink with his palms in his face,
and *he*, / the only tunnel of song for miles
in any direction.

The white belt—
Daisy and / Daisy.

And after it's over, we know we have both become men.
Him for the beating,
and me for taking his beating.

I love you, Daisy.

My father's hands will love a man / at the first sign of weakness.

I am weak / therefore, I gather that he loves me.

Their suffering
was our suffering.

They peeled the skin / off a lamb which was still breathing.

I remember its shrill cry,
but not the birria we made from it.

His hands were two doves / courting the lamb which was also a dove
in its thrashing.

They cut / through the air like ghosts.
They were large and capable / of great things.

I always came / when they called.
They always had peaches to put / in my mouth.

Rituals of Healing

Ramón, you were sick.

You weren't getting better,
but at least you were pretty.

Yes, the ticking nebula.
Yes, the machinery.

The sun performing
its ritual, swinging
its bare back across
the clockwork of sky.

You are wet and pretty.

I will believe in anything you do not
and bring it to you.

I will drink the blue night
gathered in your face
and weave your hair
for everyone watching you.

The edges of your body
touch everything
that isn't your body.

You are odorless.
      Plastic even.

      Your name is another word for fire.

What if we tell him
there's nothing wrong with him,
that he's only dying?

FIFTEEN ELEGIES

[1]
There are only masks
because we make them beautiful.

            [2]
            The sparrow—
The gold inside the sparrow.

                        [3]
                        Maybe I'm just looking for an exit.

[4]
The birds don't know it's not too late
to abandon their nests.

[5]
It was never the rain
promising us our future.

        [*Yes, I loved you most in your big brown coat.*]

        [6]
        The room was too bright—
        no one was afraid to die anymore.

            [*Serve the gin.*]

[7]
I loved the rain when it least
resembled rain.

Kissing was sometimes like that—
       when it had nothing to do with our mouths.

       [8]
       Maybe I'm not trying hard enough.

[9]
If I'm tired,
then I'm tired.

[10]
The sick were hiding—
the robes were removed from the churches
       more numinous than rain.

      [11]
      Yes, the light needs something to rest on.

      Stay still.

[12]
Let me start over.
There was a mother.

The sparrow was looking for an exit.
Kissing was sometimes like that—
       looking for an exit.

[13]
Let me start again—

     The cold disguised as a mother's hands.
     The rain.   The echo.

[14]
It was never a promise.

[15]
These are the rules you're expected to follow:

          Either praise the beautiful
          or praise what is left over.

          Choose the one that is most like a bridge.

     Soak your hands and face in it.

Immigration Interview with Jay Leno

What is your objective?
       To return all the children
       hidden behind the street lamps.

How long do you plan on staying here?
       I don't understand
       the question.

I said how long do you plan on staying here?
       We would have drowned
       even without our laughter.

Is that really your name?
       Yes, the clothes on the floor
       blossomed like the orchards in spring.

Have you been here before?
       There was a man who knew the way.
       I put his fingers in my mouth
       when he pointed in the direction of the sun.

Who are you wearing?
       The woman gave birth in the dark.
       I thought I felt hands where there were none.

       Everyone dug a useless hole.

Are you alone?
　　North was whichever way
　　the mannequins were pointing.

　　The softest bone was the one
　　that burned the longest.

Do you cry at night?
Are you alone right now?

ORIGIN OF BIRDS
—For Ramón

"The EPA estimates that roughly 20,000 farm workers are poisoned every year by pesticides, but because of many immigrants' fear of reporting incidents and inability to seek medical care, the number is likely much higher."

—Aviva Shen

"When used properly, pesticides offer a variety of benefits to society. They increase crop production, preserve produce, combat insect infestations, and control exotic species."

—Center for Disease Control

———————

You can relax because the doctor says
it's only cancer.

Yes, your hair will fall off,
and the chemo will burn.

Then all will be good, Ramón.

Remember that
those who eat alone
are holy.

―――――――――

Hair darker than deep water.

Hair climbing up the walls,
the windows,
        into our mouths, blessing us from the inside.

Eyes that can only see
        what others have already named.

        Acuario. Azucena. Colibrís.

Suddenly everything tasted
like almonds.

———————

We're trying to tip closer to the marrow.

        I close my eyes and lick your beard
and the salt of your cheek
tastes like batteries and liver.

You are the first man I have ever kissed.

When I open my eyes, everything in the room
is stained and crawling
and bruised to the touch.

It's in your blood,
       which means
       it's all of you.

Alaba:

       The blood
       that the nurses collect in jars.

Alaba:

       Your small midsection
       pale and round as the moon.

Alaba:

       The doctor's hands
       reaching into your stomach
as if looking for lost change.

Alaba:

       Even the crop duster—
       its elegant maneuverings in the sky,
       its cool mist on a hot day.

Eventually, even your milk will have to be cut
       with warm water.

A flock of birds crawled out of your mouth
    and drew the stillness outside the room.

    They pointed their beaks
    at the same time
    toward the quiet.

II.

"What You Can Know Is What You Have Made"
—*Giambattista Vico*

I want to say all of this is true
but we both know it isn't.

The song becoming
the bird becoming
the song.

Confetti for the newly fallen.

I am standing in a flower shop
to celebrate no one in particular.

What do I know of pleasure?

It's not like pouring the sun into your hair—
eyes glassy with its milk.

The bird unraveled its song and became undone.

It couldn't figure out
its own puzzle in its mouth
so it gave up.

We already know what's at the other end of this.

The bird is on the low branch
trying to put itself back together.

If only it could hold still
long enough to open and close in my palm.

Everyone in the store is like a widow
looking for her husband's face in the crowd.

                    The song
                    becoming the bird
                    becoming the song.

I imagine myself running naked through a room pretending
that I am two lamps falling over.

                    What I know of pleasure I've learned only
                    while putting my clothes back on.

I open. I close.

I am always the obedient one.
        I want this to be easy
though we know it won't.

How strange, to know this much about the future.

What's the point of any of this?

You say *open your mouth*,
so I do.

And, still, I wait.

Origin of Prayer and Eden

At first no one knew what a man or a woman really was.

They had an idea.
There was a large ripple made by a small stone.

And that was that.

Instead, everyone just swam in a river.
A wave and another wave behind it.

Eventually when we learned the vanity of prayer,
God too had to look away from himself.

We bowed our heads, not knowing to what—

We hid paper hearts in a box with all of winter's
wings beating inside.

Anything was holy
if we stared at it long enough.

How simple.

Hermosa.
Impossibility of union.

*En el agua se derramaran las preguntas de los niños
que resultan de éstas piedras.*

We pretended to be deer
pretending to play dead.

MUSICAL IN WHICH YOU AND I PLAY ALL THE ROLES

———————

This is the part of the play where the daughter brings home
        her boyfriend to meet the parents.

Let's say they're the rich and popular type.

        They like the sound the word *strengths*
        makes in their mouth.

Let's say you imagine them white
although they are not.

This is the part where her mother dips
the boy's name up and down
        like a dead bird

                hanging from a string by its feet.

I was a small thing dipped in pink
calling to the shy boys in the dark.

      —*I want to help you out of here.*   They say.

      —*Honey, you can't afford that.*   I say.

        I bobbed up to their mouth for air
        with my wide wet lips.
My name was a flesh-colored candy in their mouth.

I buried my head
        where their thighs met
           trying to peel off all of their tattoos with my tongue.

———————

We're in low light.

I'm told not to believe in you
        but I believe in the gun
        —yes even the gun.

        Yes, especially the gun we bury in the yard
        and dig up after three months of rain,
        expecting, somehow, for something
        other than a gun to blossom.

———

You bow as the lights
              go out on stage
              for the applause.

        We deserve this.

              It's completely dark
      and the audience begin clapping
but they can still hear you weeping
              and they're not sure
              whether to run up to the stage and help you
              or keep clapping.

        They keep clapping.

Essay on Synonyms for Tender and a Confession
—*For Sandra María Esteves*

Color it all blue.

      My father and my father's father and his.

      Marcelo
      Marcelo
      Marcelo

    And all of us in one suitcase that hasn't been opened.
    I haven't been opened.

        And I say to my father,
        I want to be all pink. For one day.
      To name each part of me after the names of my mother's lovers,
      To throw my head back and dance like someone pretty,
            or just hold the shame in my hand.

    And sometimes this doesn't stop me.

My name a two-hundred-year-old word for *Please*.

        As in, please let me open the suitcase.
        As in, please let me play whatever is inside.

    And sometimes my name talks to me.
              It says, *you ain't shit.*

It says *I could send you flowers but what's the point*
if they will still be flowers when you get them.

It says *even the priests are lonely.*
It comes to me as one priest confessing to another:

Marcelo, I want the red dress
and to throw my hair up real beauty queen style.

If I'm lonely, put the bright birds back in their cages.

Marcelo, I wanted a gun.
I'm not ready to be dipped in water.

Like you, like a father.

And so I opened the lid
and held each flute inside like shattered glass.

But there was no song, there was hardly any glitter.

And the priest who is no longer Marcelo,
and the flute which is no longer Marcelo,
and the lover who is.

I don't know what it means to name a child.
When he said my name, I opened his eyes.

I played the song.

Neither of us knew how it ended.
We would have paid anything at all to make it stop.

Dulce

I will gather the voices of strangers mouthing my name.

We are painting our names on each other—
colorful tattoos pushing our lungs
to the other shores of our bones.

If I could make honey
I would lie prostrate before the thief broken in half—

ribbons as the wound hurries to heal—

As large as my hand,
as large as my mouth.

We're never in much of a hurry.
It's easy to make honey from what is beautiful and what is not.

Let's imagine we live in the suburbs and call off the babysitter.
It is summer and I hardly know you.

1.
I will eat everything I love
from its edge to its center.

If it has an edge,
if it has a center.

2.
We make new friends then lose them.

3.
We never bake
another
goddamn pie again.

Either way it's a terrible future.
It's a movie where no one seems interested in the ending.

        I boil water on the stove for tea.
I am alone in the house.

I think about the cock that's never been in my mouth
to shred this kind of quiet and piece it together again.

Bi-Glyph

We made love then argued,
or, argued then made love.

It didn't matter either way,
everything had the aftertaste of gasoline.

Even the floor.
Even your hair.

We were always reaching
into each other looking for something
we didn't know we had lost.

I'm lying if I said I didn't want this.

The light barely bright enough to tear
the languor from our bodies.

The rain outside Toledo had that thick
Midwestern glue to it.

I only wanted to look far enough back
to see where I split in half.

How dumb we were
endlessly searching
for a definite shape
our longing would take.

I leaned into you,
all of you,
as if in chorus.

Azúl Nocturno: Act 1 Scene 1

Enter a man and a woman followed by entourage. They meet center stage. The setting is mid-century American modern. The stage is mostly dark save for a couch in the middle. Everyone's faces reflect a growing suspicion of general neglect. Everyone knows they are in a play.

Hello water.   Hello sweetie.
             Hello cross-legged daddy.

                     Hello cherry reds
                     drunk on the blue dial tone.

        Hello one and only unscrewing the doors off.

                        Hello anyone filming behind the white sheets
                        where the prophets gather.

Hello slick daddy.
The opposite
of *kiss* is *sick*.

            Everything's fucked the director's always saying.
            Hold your knees, like this, Rubi's always saying.

Hello river.

        Hello Blonde-Barbie.
        Hello Blonde-Ken.

You desire because you want to encounter
                    yourself desiring.

DROWN

Yes, we drowned, then changed our minds,
          then drowned again,
         because we could,
     because no one would know the difference—

        a leaf to its trembling
   when it is no longer a leaf
   but just a trembling.

        We splashed against the current—
   a zipper of palms opening and closing.

   We were too busy to notice
          that everything we touched
    was a little bell that was a little famous.

The sun opened its curfew and song

        as I swam to shake the sounds
  of your laughter off me.

Your Sweetheart, Your Scientific Theory

Dream 1.

There was a loneliness
about him
he dragged it
by the tail I opened

him It was
the first time—inside
a tangle of purple

balloons then green
then not a color at all

our mouths
moving along

the walls
of each other then
he was lonely
again He smiled
darling
limbed thing
kept unraveling yarn
beneath the cacao tree

First Gesture in Reverse

I am lying on the floor
in a pair of blue panties
that I borrowed
without telling.

Here I spread open
and become the knife
with its large smile
tilted away.

This is a star,
and this is a star.

I am thirsty.
It's called unbuckling.

I could be a bride.
Can you see it?
Aren't I a doll?

Here are my lips.
Here is the rain,
and the sound
they are capable of
inside each other.

Here the mirror
through which
I am unbearable.

The brown boy
waving the flag
of his father.
The brown boy
kissing the floor back.

If I can still close,
I will let the rain finish
what the light began
and never tell
anyone about it.

Gesture and Pursuit

I want to be the bride days later
when she is no longer a bride,
combing her hair in the mirror.

But it is too late.

I've already locked myself in my room
and imagined every variation
between witness and music.

I want everything to touch me
before it is bright enough
to slip through the house undetected—

like the sound of a child in the womb
tending its own window.

In which case anything is bright enough.

Is it too much to ask?
All I want is to run out of a church,
throw a bouquet,
and hop in a car

like my mother always wanted.

Miss Lonelyhearts

I don't know if we're doing this right,
as if right could exist between us.

We knew it would come to this—
   but we like it.

It's easy to imagine ourselves
      as loneliness tethered on a stick.
      It's easy to imagine getting used to this.

❧

We are sitting in an empty living room.
It is two in the afternoon.

   I pull my hair out one strand at a time—
         a relief at the end of my hunger.

         I wish I could be turned inside out again—
a deep purple that bone and fire make.

There's nothing more that can be done between us.

❧

      I bite the carpet until my gums bleed.
      I am not afraid of my teeth falling out,
            I am afraid of them being forgotten on the floor.

   Your menstrual blood is thick and ancient as olives or bells.

I open for you.
It feels like genuflection—
my entire body kneeling in reverence.

I'm trying to make you believe we are deer drinking water at the pond.

In the other room,
the TV has been ranting
on the same goddamn channel for three days.

Neither of us bother to turn it off.

❧

We tell each other we are pretty
and paint our name on each other's legs
with your lipstick so we can believe
it is our name.

Tell me the story
where neither of us win.

Beat me the way our parents did.
Put your belt in my mouth. Call it *Daisy*.
                I will eat it.
                I will make it come back to life.

I promise.

❧

We can live out the rest of our lives like this.

Let's play house.
For now I will play the man and you will play the woman.
Or you will play the man and I will play the woman.

You pull a child
        from between your legs that will not cut you.

        But it will die,
as they all have.
It will be still,

forever
only once in its life.

Nuclear Fictions

We are completely miserable
but no one can tell
from the smiles on our faces.

Everyone is watching us on TV from home.
They think it's a show about foxes.

They know we know.
We bow to the image of their desire.

It's a game where the plastic is missing.
The world keeps coming
in and out of our coats.

So we give them a show.

Here, the hummingbird
flushed in a cool electric drizzle.

We run home in the rain
because we are banal.
We replay our childhood
braided among the apple trees.

Then the morning, then puberty,
then coffee before headed to work.
Then the cream-colored walls,
cheap red lipstick through a dirty mirror.

This is the way you look at me
when we are going nowhere.

To them there's always a man on the left
walking away from a woman.
There's always a woman on the right
walking away from a man.

Sometimes I can't tell if the cameras are on.
We nod our obedient heads.

Let them watch.
Let the sun sink to the surface of someone else's sky.

If we leave our bodies now,
they will find their way back to us eventually.
They always do.

Until then, touch me, I am gentle.
This has nothing to do with the rain.

Let's lean into the creek
and stare at ourselves in the water,
and wash our faces before we drown in them.

Sub-Erotica Papers

Your body was the darkest thing on me
        filled with panic and thirst.

At last you opened my eyes and said

look at me,
look at me Goddamnit.

    So I did.

Neither of us knew
what we wanted
but would do anything
to have it.

You said
I want to believe it is art
even if we don't change.

                ❧

        We took off our clothes
and fucked each other in front of our friends.
        We wanted them to watch
and throw flowers at us.
We wanted to be angry at something
                that we could name.

I ran through the streets yelling
        get it while it's hot.
        You kept predicting the future.
        It was something like this.

Our friends applauded.

We bowed.

The judges asked to see it again,
             but we didn't know how
    so we burned the fields
    and the cattle died.

        ❧

In the end, what did I know about touching a woman
with the same hands I used to cut grapes?
What did I know about touching a man?

        ❧

Have we barely begun our departure?

        Dear judges,
        none of you can imagine
        the incredible amount of money
        it costs to be poor.

First Wedding Dance

The music stopped playing years ago
but we're still dancing.

There's your bright skirt scissoring
through the crowd—

our hips tipping the instruments over.

You open me up and walk inside
until you reach a river
where a child is washing her feet.

You aren't sure
if I am the child
or if I am the river.

You throw a stone
and the child wades in to find it.
This is memory.

Let's say the river is too deep
so you turn around and leave
the same way you entered—
spent and unwashed.

It's ok. We are young, and
our gowns are as long as the room.

I told you I always wanted a silk train.

We can both be the bride,
we can both empty our lover.

And there's nothing different about you—
about me—about any of this.
Only that we wish it still hurt, just once.

Like the belts our fathers whipped us with,
not to hurt us but just to make sure we remembered.

Like the cotton ball, dipped in alcohol,
rubbed gently on your arm
moments before the doctor asks you to breathe.

Pulling the Moon

I've never made love to a man.
I've never made love to a man but I imagine.

        I imagine pulling the moon.
        I imagine pulling the moon out of his brow.

Pulling the moon out of his brow and eating it again.

        Eating and pulling his hair in silence.
A kind of silence when the moon goes out.

When the moon goes back and forth between us.

A kind of silence lit for only a moment.
Seeing for a moment through the eyes of the horse.

        Through the eyes of the dead horse
        that burns slower than my hair.

My hair that burns the moon off.
My hair with a hand inside it.

HOW TO GROW THE BRIGHTEST GERANIUM

———————

I am not ashamed

the story goes

I swear I will learn

to leave a room

without touching

every part of your face

III.

ORIGIN OF THEFT

———————

The doctor reached in
        and pulled out the child
   as if holding
   a small shard of glass.

       Anything can cut you.
       You can never be too careful.

You drew small circles in the sheets with your finger.
       So calm. So slow.

The knocking
was a thief saying

I'm sorry,
I'm so sorry.

There's nothing else I can take.

I dragged all the sheets I could find through the hallway.
This made sense to me at one point.

Everything reflected in the doorknob
was upside down and in reverse,
as if it never happened.

The bones
unhinged at the same speed
as the branches.

May the children climb the trees.
   May we learn their symmetry.

  May they turn away from us
  as we model their grief.

  May they model our grief.
May they bloom flowers from the tips
   of their fingers.

  Turn that autumn red.

  We will make tea from the flowers
and their hearts will grow as large
  as our wet palms
  in the sink.

The story goes something like this.

The leaves pass the wind to each other
and all at once the tree is one complete shudder.

It's simple, says my father.

The light through the window—unremarkable.
The lace curtains—unremarkable.

The roots know winter is coming
long before the branches.

All the bills were sent to collections.

It is possible to only see things that have been given names.

> You saw the child
> but didn't know
> what to call her.

> Read me the story
> that doesn't end with the drowning.

> *The orchards were late to bloom that year.*
> *Everything was a mimicry of itself.*

———————

Can we go back far enough?
Let's reimagine a house.

Remarkable.

We each have part of the story memorized—
    First was the failure of expectations.

It was the same child
coming back again and again.

You gave her your teeth.
You gave her your hair.

        No.
You gave her everything.

An act on the body
        is only a cure
        if it happens
more than once—
otherwise we call it a miracle.

Santisima Madre.
We call you by the names of your believers.

    So we knew the child was either cured
    or holy.

The story goes something like this:
There was a man rattling some change in a can.

    I wanted to love him.
    I wanted to tell him the story.

I made plans in my head.
Played make-believe.
There was hardly any salt on his fingers.

LOVE POEM: A NOCTURNE

I cut the cord and
split you from the child.

And when I looked down,
in one hand I held a bowl of water,
        a small bell that couldn't ring
        in the other.

            I poured the water
                    over the bell and listened.

Half of you raptured in song,
            the other half

        a biography of grief
        wholly unknown to me—
        a sea of individual tremblings.

For love, I would separate
your body from the light
that wraps around you.

            I've thought of naming her Azucena:
            little wet bell.

            I will keep her name in a jar
                    and wait for her to grow up and laugh
            when I open the lid and tell her
            this is where you came from.

GESTURE WITH BOTH HANDS TIED

I'm going to open the borders of my hunger
and call it a parade.

But I'm lying if I said I was hungry.

If dying required practice,
I could give up the conditions for being alone.

I undress in the sun and stare at it
until I can stand its brightness no longer.

Why is it always noon in my head?

I'm going to run outside and whisper,
or hold a gun and say *bang*,

or hold a gun and not do anything at all.

The lamps that wait inside me say
come, the gift is the practice,
the price is the door.

"You Must Sing to Be Found; When Found, You Must Sing."
—*Li-Young Lee*

Another doctor
pulled another child from you
and gave it to me.

He was gentle.
He was better than any knife.

Your one good dress
in my one good hand
in the only light.

We closed our eyes
and looked for each other.

The doctor was laughing,
and we were laughing,
and the babies were laughing.

We forgot in which direction to point
the living world
when it came
stumbling toward us.

We pressed our ears to the ground
and listened to the bells
in the throats of the dead.

Everyone thought they could hear
the sounds of children playing
when in fact

they all walked into a tree
and never came back out.

Rima: Notes and Observations

We have lost so much time.

> I am naked in the river.
> Our eyes are larger than visible things.

We're broken the way things should be broken.

> As Christ did, we did.
> We knew how to touch.

[Risen.]

Our clothes are wet.

> Every blue center cut
> > out of every blue center.
>
> Don't you understand?
> They will never dry.

[Risen.]

I can't tell you what other name to call it.

> Consider the octopus.
> If you too had three hearts
> would you

want one to keep you alive
while the other two split you in half?

[*Rise.*]

Origin of Glass

[gesture and arabesque]

It is winter again
as we feel our way through
a bed of glass beneath the water.

> We've been here before,
> everything's the same—
>
> still the morning,
> still the sharp pieces of glass
> we pile into a sculpture of a child and praise.

In truth we can't
make anything happen between us.

> Winter began
> with her hands detached from the branches.
>
> No one knew,
> but I knew.

[gesture of the displaced]

I want to believe this will end
with thousands watching
and throwing roses at us,
        with lights and glitter in our hair.

But we both know how it ends—

we practice it over and over until we don't
need to tell our bodies how to do it.

[gesture with the sound of a bell in it]

Will you hold her to the light?
Will you breathe a little pink into her?

Not everything is a bright flute
made of bone.

I'm convinced she is a swarm of honey bees.

What if they died not because they stung
but because they grew tired of stinging?

[gesture with an error in its name]

You washed the sand out of your hair,
where the mushrooms outnumbered the stars.

I sat in the sun near the river
and quietly rolled clay between my legs.

Winter began like this.

O, its constellation.
Its jeweled pity.

You knew,
you always knew.

NOTES

Cenzontle means mockingbird in Spanish and comes from the Nahuatl word *centzuntli,* which refers to one who holds 400 voices or songs.

As the epigraph indicates, "Origin of Birds" is dedicated to my late uncle, Ramón Hernandez Gonzalez, who died of cancer due to extreme exposure to pesticides and fertilizers regularly used in agriculture, which workers come in contact with on a daily basis. The line "those who eat alone are holy" is from Cathy Park Hong's poem "A Wreathe of Hummingbirds."

The title "What You Can Know Is What You Have Made" refers to the 17th-century Italian Philosopher Giambattista Vico's idea of the *Verum Factum Principle*, which states that "Man makes himself the measure of all things." This poem also uses a logical structure modified from Kathleen Graber's book *Eternal City*.

Larry Levis's voice is ever-present throughout this book. "Origin of Prayer and Eden," in particular, was imagined after Levis's phrase "even a horse's hoof is holy." "Origin of Drowning or Crossing the Rio Bravo" also borrows a phrase, "brimming over with extinct love," from Levis.

"Origin of Prayer and Eden" uses a line from W. S. Merwin's poem "For the Anniversary of My Death."

The lines "everything we touched / was a little bell that was a little famous" in the poem "Drown" are adapted from a poem by Brenda Hillman, who helped me begin that poem and to whom I am grateful.

"Miss Lonelyhearts" owes its ending to Peter Marcus.

"Nuclear Fictions" and "Origin of Glass" rely on Tomas Tranströmer's book *For the Living and the Dead* for parts of its structure and borrow some of its language.

"Sub-Erotica Papers" ends with lines by César Vallejo from his book *Trilce*.

ACKNOWLEDGMENTS

I am grateful to the editors of the following journals and anthologies who saw something in these poems which have since changed dramatically in their original form or title but nonetheless, a small something in them continues:

Break Water Review: "How to Grow the Brightest Geranium" and "Azul Nocturno: Act 1 Scene 1";

Clade Song: "Musical in Which You and I Play All the Roles";

The Collagist: "Origin of Prayer and Eden";

Construction Magazine: "Love Poem: A Nocturne" and "Your Sweetheart, Your Scientific Theory";

Devil's Lake: "Origin of Drowning or Crossing the Rio Bravo" and sections of "Origin of Birds";

Drunken Boat: "Origin of Theft";

Four Way Review: "Origin of Glass";

Gulf Coast: A Journal of Literature and Fine Arts: "Wetback" and "Century of Good Metal with Three Prayers";

Huizache: "El Frutero" and sections of "Sub-Erotica Papers";

Indiana Review: "Gesture and Pursuit";

The Journal: sections of "Origin of Birds";

Luna Luna: "Bi-Glyph" and "'You Must Sing to Be Found; When Found, You Must Sing.'";

Muzzle Magazine: "Immigration Interview with Don Francisco";

Nepantla: a Journal for Queer Poets of Color: "Drown";

New England Review: "Rituals of Healing" and "Pulling the Moon";

Southern Humanities Review: "What You Can Know Is What You Have Made";

The Notre Dame Review: "Gesture with Both Hands Tied" and sections of "Chronology of Undocumented Mothers";

The Offending Adam: "Dulce" and sections of "Chronology of Undocumented Mothers";

The Ostrich Review: "Dear Ramon";

The Paris American: "Cenzontle";

Rhino Poetry: "First Gesture in Reverse";

Toe Good Literary Journal: sections of "Origin of Birds";

Winter Tangerine: section of "Chronology of Undocumented Mothers."

"Cenzontle" appears in the anthology *Nepantla: An Anthology for Queer Poets of Color*, Nightboat Books, ed. by Christopher Soto.

"Cenzontle" was translated into Spanish by Mariana Rodríguez and reprinted in *Mexico City Lit*.

"Sugar," "El Frutero," and "Origin of Prayer and Eden" were translated into Spanish by Francisco Larios and appear in the anthology *Los Hijos de Whitman: Poesía Norteamericana del siglo XXI*, Valparaíso Ediciones Mexico.

"Essay on Synonyms for Tender and a Confession" appears in the anthology *Bettering American Poetry 2015*.

"Sub-Erotica Papers" appears in *Wingbeats II Anthology*, Dos Gatos Press, ed. by Scott Wiggerman and David Meischen.

"Immigration Interview with Don Francisco" was reprinted in *PBS NewsHour*, article by Corinne Segal.

This book would not exist without the unwavering support and care from people who have given me the gift of friendship and intellectual rigor. For all the fires we have started, my endless gratitude and love to Suzi F. Garcia, Derrick Austin, Vanessa Angélica Villarreal, and Rob Bruno. May we have endless light. To Lauren Clark, we are alive at the same time, thank you.

Thank you to Eduardo C. Corral and Francisco Aragón, who challenged me to take the next leap a long time ago. For their insights, encouragement, advice, and care, thank you to Gabrielle Calvocoressi, Tarfia Faizullah, Carolina Ebeid, Rosebud Ben-Oni, David Campos, C. Dale Young, Nate Marshall, Kazim Ali, Ruben Quesada, ire'ne lara silva, Rigoberto González, Cathy Park Hong, Brit Bennett, Yesenia Montilla, Erika L. Sánchez, and Lisette Chavez for creating the stunning lithograph on the cover. Un fuerte abrazo to the BOA family, especially to Peter Conners, Ron Martin-Dent, Kelly Hatton, and Sandy Knight. Mi cariño y eterno agradecimiento a Brenda Shaughnessy for selecting my poems and giving them a home. Gracias.

I am grateful to the generosity of Helen Zell and the MFA program at the University of Michigan for providing me the time and support to dedicate myself to this book. Thank you to my teachers Keith Taylor, Lorna Goodison, Linda Gregerson, A. Van Jordan, David M. Halperin, and especially Laura Kasischke. A special thanks to those at Sacramento State who believed in me very early on; thank you to Josh McKinney, Hellen Lee, Brad Buchanan, and Nancy Sweet. Great appreciation extends to the gifts of time and camaraderie at the Vermont Studio Center, the Squaw Valley Community of Writers, and the Atlantic Center for the Arts. Thank you Lisa Alvarez, Brett Hall Jones, John Murillo, Nicole Sealey, Ren Morrison, and Kelle Groom.

I owe so much to my CantoMundo familia. I am forever grateful to you for letting me be vulnerable and never lonely. Mil gracias a Celeste Guzmán Mendoza, Deborah Paredez, Norma Elia Cantú, and especially to Carmen Giménez Smith for teaching me to be an accomplice. I am forever grateful to Natalie Scenters-Zapico for reordering and envisioning the final structure of this book.

Shout out to Undocupoets who helped change the game, including this A. Poulin, Jr. Prize. My love to Javier Zamora, Christopher Soto (aka Loma), Janine Joseph, and all those to come. May we continue to fight.

Adelante C. D. Wright. Thank you for showing me a path to the language of my origin. I will never be the same. Que en paz descanses. My sincerest gratitude to my family who were the first poets I learned from, Yole, Sergio, Danny, and Gilberto. To my parents Antonia y Marcelo, al fin estamos juntos todos.

And finally, my abiding and endless love to Rubi and my son Julián whom I dedicate this book to. Julián, when you are born, I will open a jar and tell you where your name came from.

ABOUT THE AUTHOR

Marcelo Hernandez Castillo is a poet, essayist, translator and Canto Mundo Fellow born in Tepechitlan Zacatecas, México. He studied at Sacramento State University as an AB 540 student and was the first undocumented student to graduate from the Helen Zell Writers Program at the University of Michigan. He is the winner of the 6th annual Drinking Gourd Chapbook Prize from Northwestern University Press, and his memoir is forthcoming from HarperCollins Publishers. He cofounded the Undocupoets campaign, which successfully eliminated citizenship requirements from all major first book poetry prizes in the country, and was recognized with the Barnes & Noble Writers for Writers award from *Poets & Writers*. He has been featured in the *New York Times*, *BuzzFeed*, *Fusion TV*, *PBS NewsHour*, and his poems have appeared in *New England Review*, *Gulf Coast*, *Indiana Review*, and *Southern Humanities Review*, among others. He lives in California.

BOA Editions, Ltd.
The A. Poulin, Jr. New Poets of America Series

COLOPHON

BOA Editions, Ltd., a not-for-profit publisher of poetry and other literary works, fosters readership and appreciation of contemporary literature. By identifying, cultivating, and publishing both new and established poets and selecting authors of unique literary talent, BOA brings high-quality literature to the public. Support for this effort comes from the sale of its publications, grant funding, and private donations.

❧

The publication of this book is made possible, in part,
by the support of the following patrons:

Anonymous
Angela Bonazinga & Catherine Lewis
Reginald Gibbons
Robert L. Giron
Keetje & Sarah Kuipers
Jack & Gail Langerak
LGBT Fund for Greater Rochester
Melanie & Ron Martin-Dent
Joe McElveney
Boo Poulin
Deborah Ronnen & Sherman Levey
Steven O. Russell & Phyllis Rifkin-Russell
William Waddell & Linda Rubel
Michael Waters & Mihaela Moscaliuc
Tom White & Kelly Hatton